Bastien® New Traditions

All In One
PIANO COURSE

BY LISA, LORI, & JANE BASTIEN

MW00534615

Level

LESSONS
THEORY
TECHNIC
PERFORMANCE

Illustrations by **Ying-Hwa Hu**

ISBN-10: 0-8497-9788-8
ISBN-13: 978-0-8497-9788-0

Dear Teachers and Parents:

Bastien New Traditions: All In One Piano Course is a captivating and dynamic method designed for student achievement and success. It combines the successful, time-tested Bastien piano pedagogy with new teaching ideas and techniques. Stemming from our many years of experience teaching students of diverse abilities and interests, we have developed this engaging curriculum for today's busy students.

Features include:

- **All-in-one books** with lesson, technic, theory, and performance pages fully integrated in each book for a streamlined, comprehensive, easy-to-use approach.

- **Appropriate reinforcement** and pacing throughout to ensure success for students with diverse abilities and interests.

- **Innovative, gradual multi-key** approach blended with intervallic reading. Staff reading begins with Middle C using varied hand placements, as well as traditional 5-finger positions.

- **Captivating music**, featuring outstanding solo pieces and duet accompaniments, an excellent variety of different musical styles, and an abundance of familiar melodies to inspire students.

- **Holistic approach** to concepts integrating elements of lessons, theory, technic, and performance.

- **Inviting pages**, beautifully organized and clutter-free, with stunning watercolor illustrations.

- **Technology** included in every book designed to assist practice and motivate students.

Learning to play the piano is an enriching and joyful experience. We wish you much success in your student's musical journey!

Neil A. Kjos Music Company
Lisa Bastien
Lori Bastien
Jane Smisor Bastien

Essential Supplementary Materials for Level 1B:

Bastien Assignment Book (KP50)

Naming Accidentals (KP29)
Intervals Through a Fifth (KP26)
Lines and Spaces Note Speller (KP23)

Bastien Music Flashcards (GP27)
The daily use of music flashcards is highly recommended to aid in recognizing individual notes. Each time new notes are introduced, numbered miniature flashcards are included on the page. These numbers correspond with the Bastien *Music Flashcards* (GP27). Find and separate the numbered cards from your set of music flashcards. Name, play, and memorize these new notes.

Contents

3

WP453

REFERENCE and REVIEW

The Notes On the Staff and Keyboard

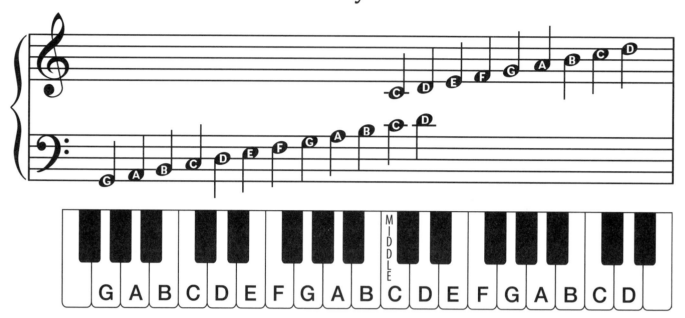

Intervals

Interval – the distance between two notes.

Melodic intervals are single notes played one at a time, like notes in a melody.

2nd   3rd   4th   5th

Harmonic intervals are two notes played together to make harmony in music.

2nd   3rd   4th   5th

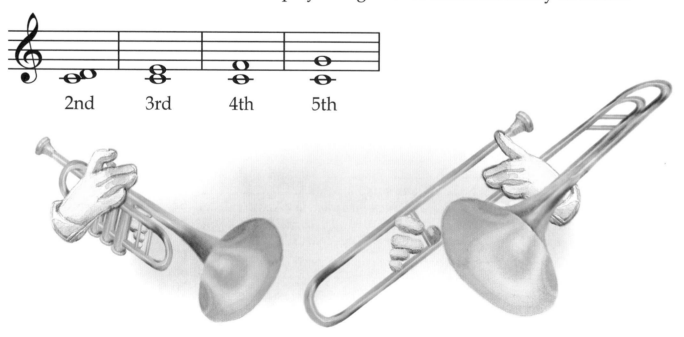

Sharps and Flats

Tempo Marks

Andante	Walking tempo
Moderato	Moderate
Allegretto	Moderately fast
Allegro	Fast

The sharp sign (♯) in music means to play the next key to the right, which may be either black or white.

 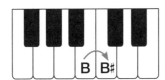 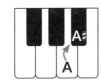

The flat sign (♭) in music means to play the next key to the left, which may be either black or white.

  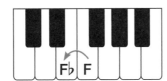

Stem Rule

Notes on or above the middle staff line have **down stems**. Notes below the middle staff line have **up stems**.

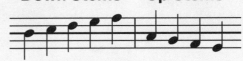

Terms		Meanings
Slur		A curved line over or under two or more different notes that are to be played *legato* (smooth and connected).
Phrase		A phrase is a musical thought. A line similar to a slur is often used to show a phrase.
Tie		A curved line that connects notes on the same line or space. The first note is played and held through the value of the second note.
Staccato		Play short, separated notes.
Upbeat(s)		Note(s) that come before the first full measure of a piece.
Crescendo	*cresc.*	Gradually play louder.
Diminuendo	*dim.*	Gradually play softer.
Ritardando	*rit.*	Gradually slow down.
8ᵛᵃ		Play the notes one octave higher or lower.
15ᵐᵃ		Play the notes two octaves higher or lower.

RH 5 begins on ___.
LH 1 begins on ___.

Westminster Chimes

Andante

Traditional English Tune

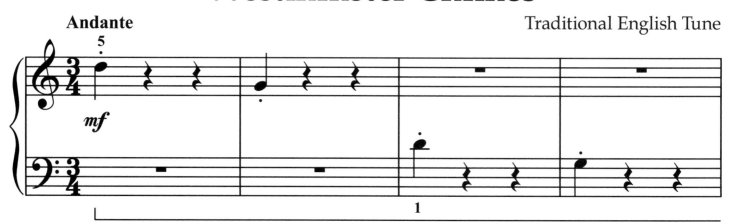

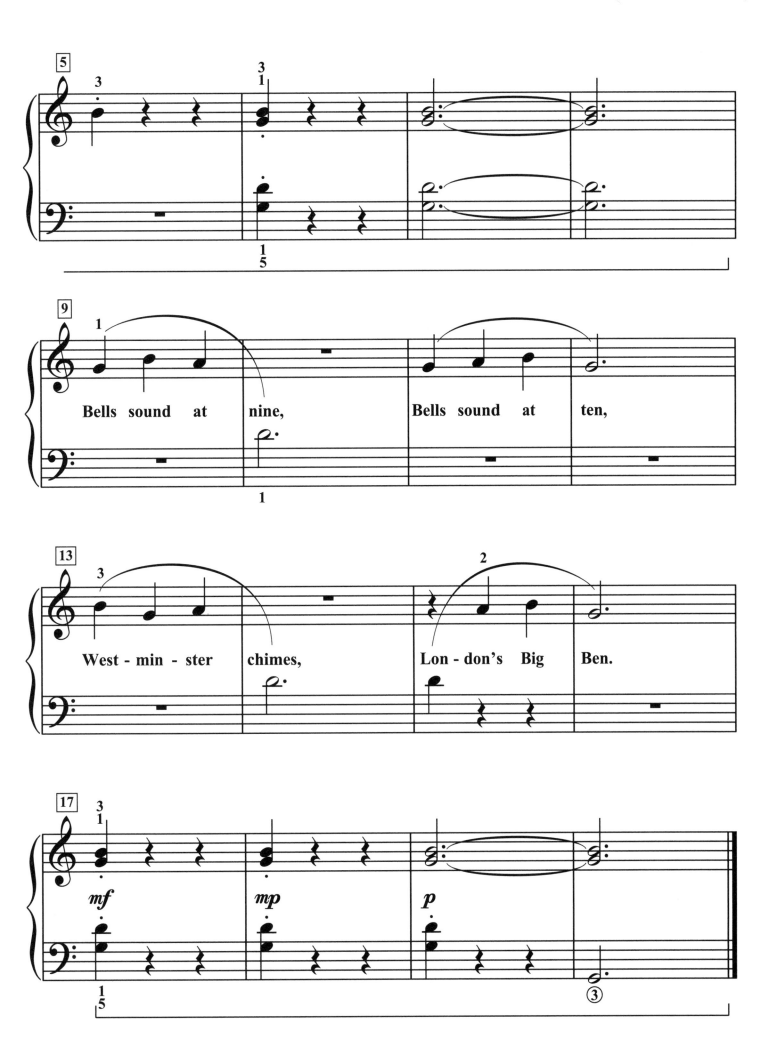

Bass Clef Line Notes

A. Write the note names inside the noteheads.

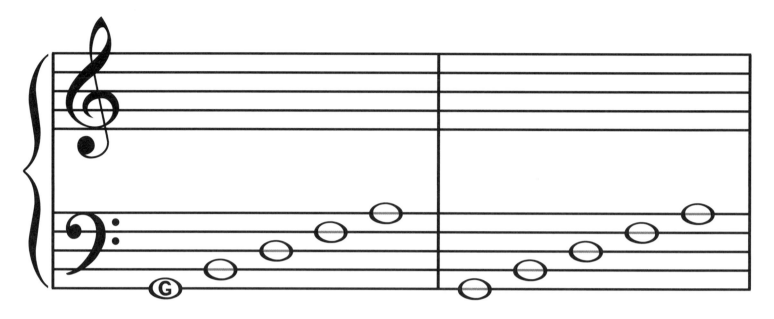

B. Write a saying for the bass clef line notes to help you remember the letter names.
   An example: **G**rown **B**aby **D**ucks **F**ly **A**way

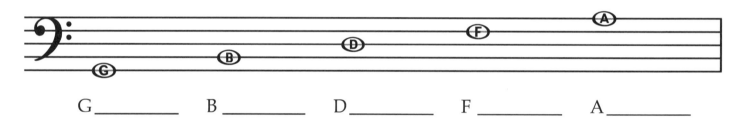

G_____   B_____   D_____   F_____   A_____

C. Name these line notes.

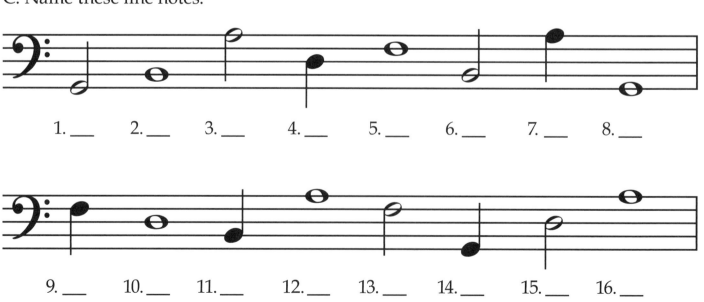

1. ___   2. ___   3. ___   4. ___   5. ___   6. ___   7. ___   8. ___

9. ___   10. ___   11. ___   12. ___   13. ___   14. ___   15. ___   16. ___

LH 5 begins on ___.

RH 5 begins on ___.

RH 1 begins on ___.

Electric Guitar

You are ready for **Naming Accidentals** (KP29).

WP453

Two Eighth Notes:

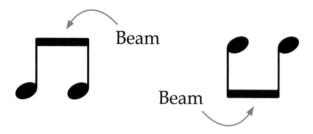 = ♩ = 1 beat in **2/4**, **3/4**, and **4/4**

½ + ½ = 1

Beam

Beam

Example: Clap and count aloud.

2/4 ♩ ♫♩ | ♩
  1 + 2 +   1 + 2 +

A. Trace the eighth notes, then draw two more sets of each.

B. Write the counts on the gray line under the notes, then clap and count each example.

1 + 2 +

C. Complete these "music math" problems.

♫ + ¿ + ♩ + ♩

☐ + ☐ + ☐ + ☐ = ☐ beats

o + ♫ + ▬ + ♩.

☐ + ☐ + ☐ + ☐ = ☐ beats

RH 2 begins on ___.
LH 1 begins on ___.

Skip to My Lou

American Folk Song

Accompaniment

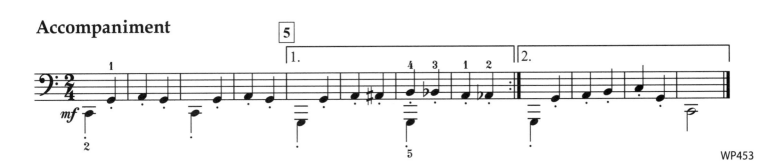

Clap and count the rhythm aloud.

A **fermata** sign ⌒ indicates a pause in music. Hold the note or notes under a fermata sign longer than their original time value.

LH 3 begins on ___.
RH 1 begins on ___.

Happy Birthday

Words by
Patty and Mildred Hill

Moderato

mf Hap-py Birth-day to you. Hap-py Birth-day to you. Hap-py

Birth - day dear ___ ___, Hap-py Birth - day to you.

Hold

ACCOMPANIMENT (Student plays one octave higher)

RH 2 begins on ___.
LH 4 begins on ___.

Minuet in G

Christian Petzold
(Arranged)

Allegretto

mf Bach liked this lit - tle mel - o - dy. It's called the Min - u - et in G.

Great el - e-gance and charm ring out in each note of this cheer-ful, bright tune.

This clas - sic piece from old - en times still bright-ens up our hearts and minds.

Dance-like and play - ful, clear, light and sim-ple, here's Min - u - et in G.

Rhythm Review

A. Add a note to each box to complete the rhythm.

B. Clap and count the rhythm aloud.

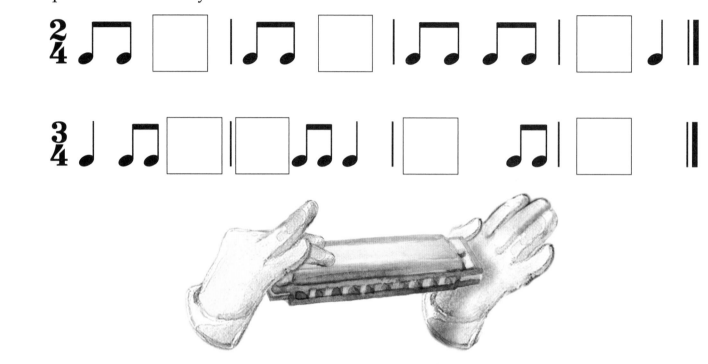

Harmonic Workout

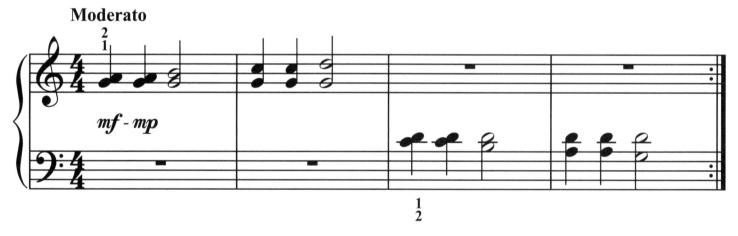

Melodic Workout

Rhythm Review

A. Write the counts on the gray line below the rhythm.
B. Clap and count the rhythm aloud.

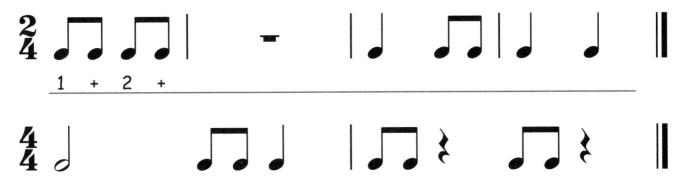

LH 5 begins on ____.
RH 1 begins on ____.

Water Slide

Moderato

Bass Clef Space Notes

A. Write the note names inside the noteheads.

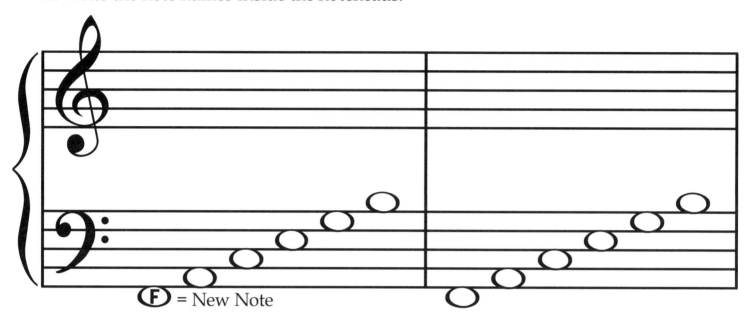

F = New Note

B. Write a saying for the bass clef space notes to help you remember the letter names. Example: **F**irst **A**ll **C**ows **E**at **G**rass **B**oldly. The first four bass clef space notes spell the word "face."

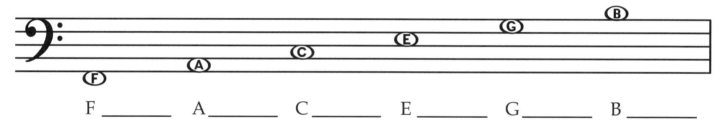

F _____   A _____   C _____   E _____   G _____   B _____

C. Name these space notes.

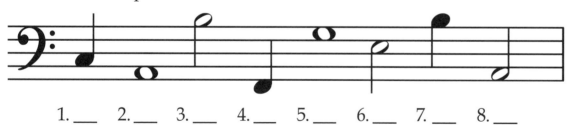

1. __   2. __   3. __   4. __   5. __   6. __   7. __   8. __

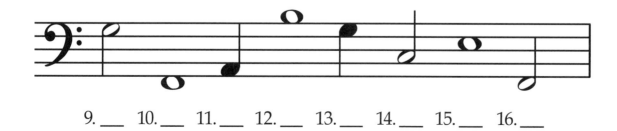

9. __   10. __   11. __   12. __   13. __   14. __   15. __   16. __

New Note

Beaming Eighth Notes

Eighth notes may be grouped in 2's or 4's.

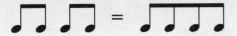

Clap and count aloud.

LH 2 begins on ____
RH 4 begins on ____.

Scottish Bluebells

Moderato

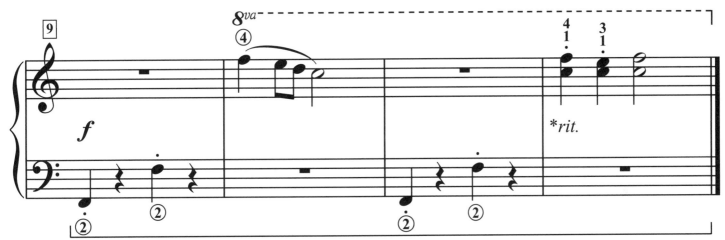

*Abbreviation of *ritardando*. Gradually slow down.

18

LH 1 begins on ___.

LH 3 begins on ___.

RH 3 begins on ___.

Before I Sleep

Traditional Lullaby Tune

Andante

mp - p Some-times if sleep won't come eas-i- ly, I will lie in bed, think-ing

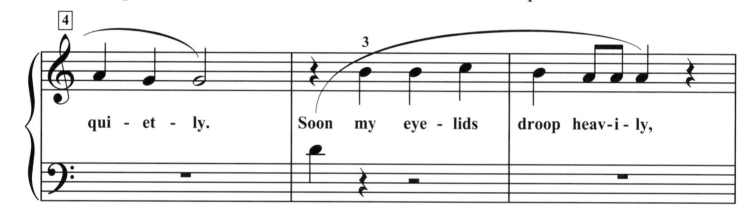

qui - et - ly. Soon my eye - lids droop heav-i- ly,

Then I fall a-sleep dream-ing peace - ful - ly. *p*

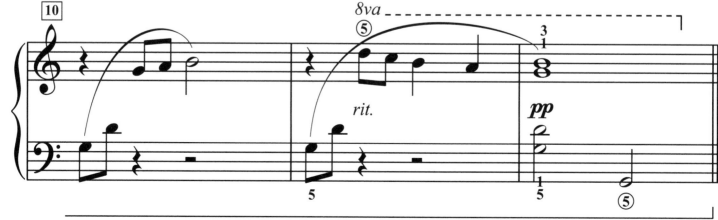

rit. *pp*

WP453

Practice Directions (measures 1 and 2):
1. Play hands separately first.
2. Play hands together slowly, listening for a singing legato RH and a soft staccato LH.

RH 5 begins on ___.

LH 1 begins on ___.
LH 5 begins on ___.

Musette

Johann Sebastian Bach
(Arranged)

* Music often shows that one hand is to be played legato while the other hand is to be played staccato. Mastering this technic takes time, concentration, and slow practice.

Name the notes.

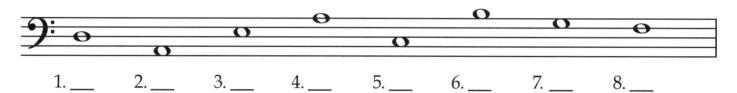

1. __ 2. __ 3. __ 4. __ 5. __ 6. __ 7. __ 8. __

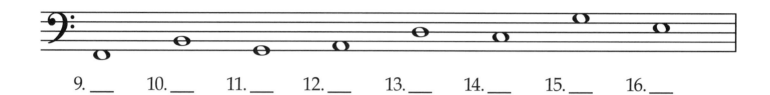

9. __ 10. __ 11. __ 12. __ 13. __ 14. __ 15. __ 16. __

LH 1 begins on ___.

Diving Under the Sea

Name the notes.

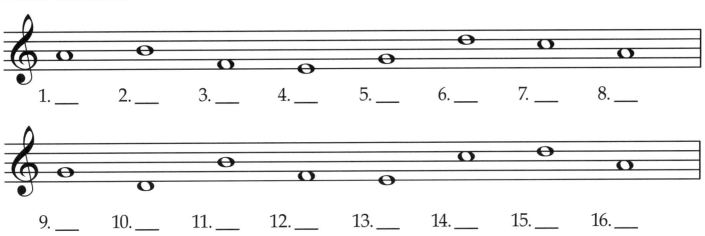

1. __ 2. __ 3. __ 4. __ 5. __ 6. __ 7. __ 8. __

9. __ 10. __ 11. __ 12. __ 13. __ 14. __ 15. __ 16. __

RH 1 begins on ___.

Riding the Waves

Moderato

Space E Line F Space G

A. Draw each note three times.

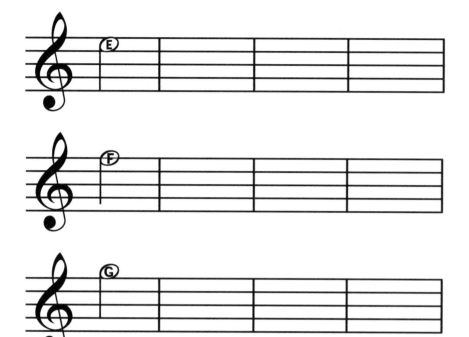

B. Name these guide notes.

High G is another important **guide note**.

C. Name the notes.

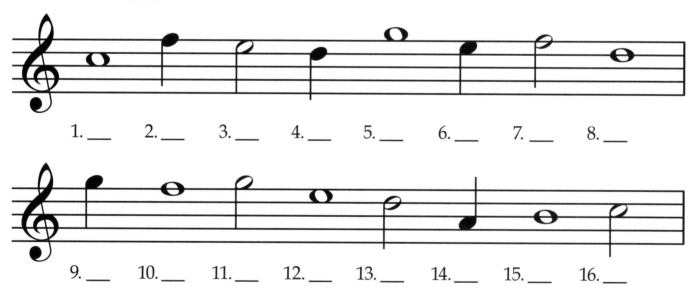

1. __ 2. __ 3. __ 4. __ 5. __ 6. __ 7. __ 8. __

9. __ 10. __ 11. __ 12. __ 13. __ 14. __ 15. __ 16. __

New Notes

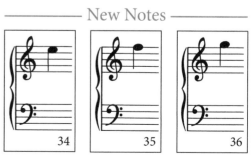

You are ready for **Intervals Through A Fifth** (KP26).

C 5-Finger Position (Treble C)

Lions and Lionesses

Moderato

mf 1. Li - o - ness - es   hunt   for the   food to feed their   fam - 'lies,
f 2. Li - ons learn to   roar   a fer -   o - cious sound-ing   bel - low,

First they serve their   mates,   then they   feed their cubs, "Hoo-   ray!"
Li - ons can be   heard   up to   five long miles a -   way.

mp

Interval Review

Name the notes, then circle the interval name.

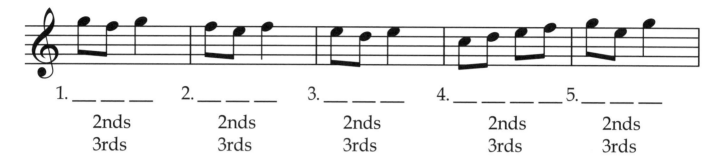

1. __ __ __   2. __ __ __   3. __ __ __   4. __ __ __ __   5. __ __ __

| 2nds | 2nds | 2nds | 2nds | 2nds |
| 3rds | 3rds | 3rds | 3rds | 3rds |

6. __ __ __ __   7. __ __ __ __   8. __ __ __ __   9. __ __ __ __

| 2nds | 2nds | 2nds | 2nds |
| 3rds | 3rds | 3rds | 3rds |

Rhythm Review

Add one note to complete each measure. Clap and count the rhythm aloud.

Crescendo (⟍) means to gradually play louder.
Decrescendo/Diminuendo (⟋) means to gradually play softer.

RH 1 begins on ___.
LH 1 begins on ___.

Dance of the Swans

Soccer Party

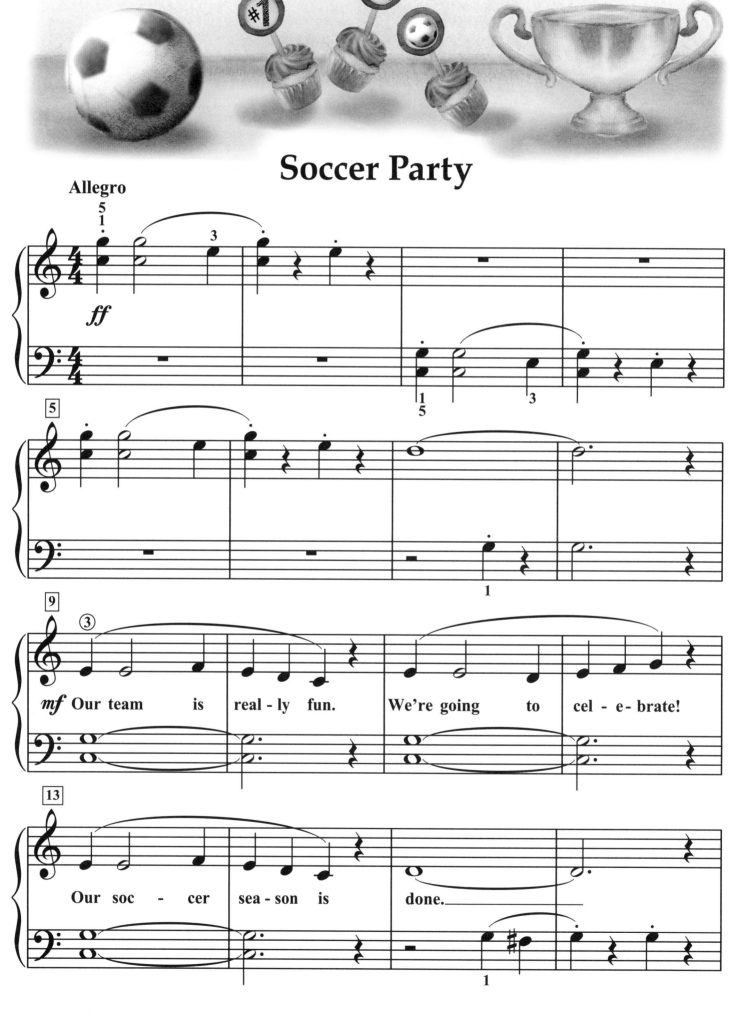

Join us at four o'-clock, We'll have a bar-be-que!

Our team is num - ber one!_____

ff

8va_____

I Chord

In the C 5-finger position:

- The **C chord** is built on C, the **tonic note.**
- The C chord is also called the **tonic chord** or the **I chord** (pronounced "one chord").
- The notes of the C chord are **C – E – G.**

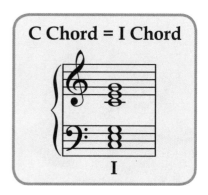

RH 1 begins on ___.
LH 5 begins on ___.

C Chord Prelude

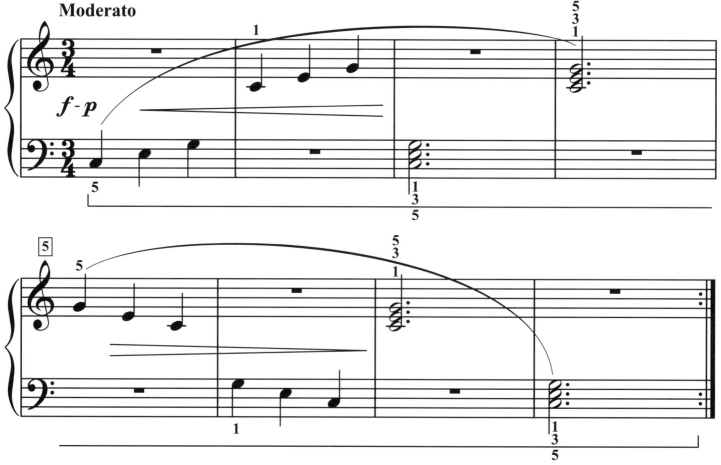

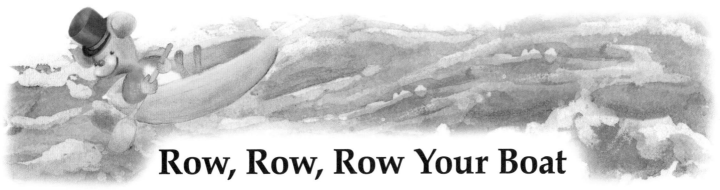

Row, Row, Row Your Boat

Allegretto

American Folk Song

mf Row, row, row your boat,

Gent - ly down the stream.

Mer - ri - ly, mer - ri - ly, mer - ri - ly, mer - ri - ly,

Life is but a dream.

*Listen for soft LH chords.

WP453

Two-Note V7 Chord

In the C 5-finger position:
- The two-note **V7 chord** (pronounced "five-seven chord") is made up of the 4th and 5th notes.
- The notes of the **V7** chord are **F** and **G**. (Later, you will learn **V7** chords that have additional notes.)

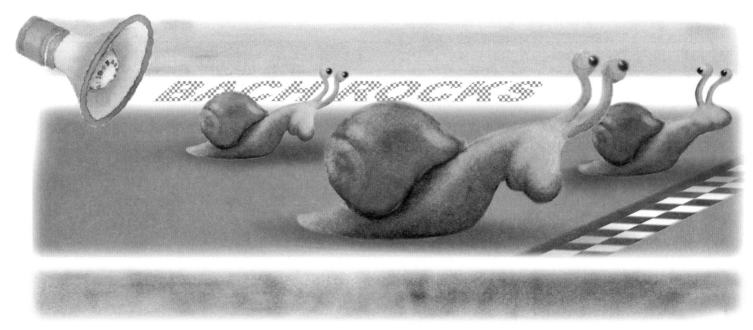

Go Team!

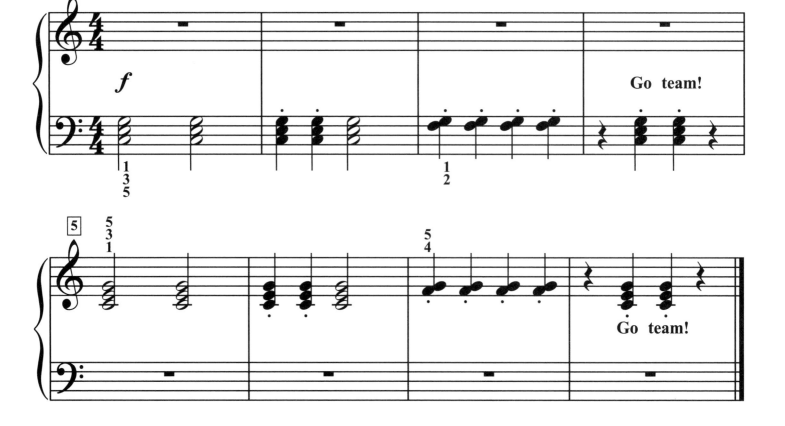

Snail Friends

Andante

mp Near my house, two snails met, they were ver - y small.

In straight lines, took their time, crawl-ing up our wall.

p   *rit.*   *pp*

Drawing I and V7 Chords

1. **I** = "one chord"
   Draw three **I** chords.

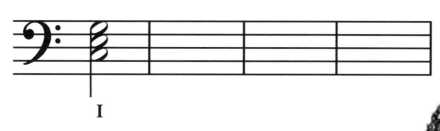

I

2. **V7** = "five-seven chord"
   Draw three **V7** chords.

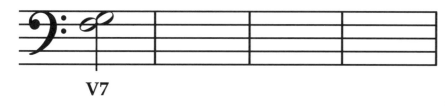

V7

Write the chord names (**I** or **V7**) in the boxes.

Chord Etude

Note Review

A. Name the notes.

B. Write the number of each note on the matching key below.

1. _C_ 2. __ 3. __ 4. __ 5. __ 6. __ 7. __ 8. __

Waltz of the Butterflies

Moderato

Play RH 8va higher on repeat

Play the LH chords quietly.

School Carnival

*A barline cancels an accidental (sharp or flat).

D.C. al Fine

WP453

Treble Clef Line Notes

A. Write the note names inside the noteheads.

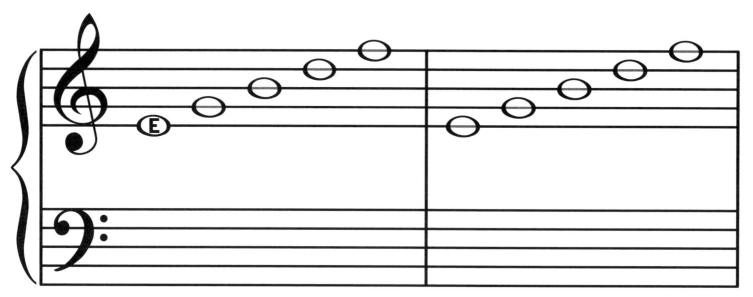

B. Write a saying for the treble clef line notes to help you remember the letter names.
Example: **E**ggs **G**et **B**roken **D**uring **F**lipping.

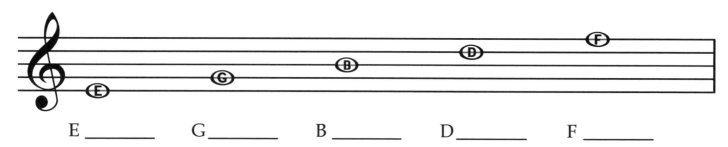

E _____   G _____   B _____   D _____   F _____

C. Name these line notes.

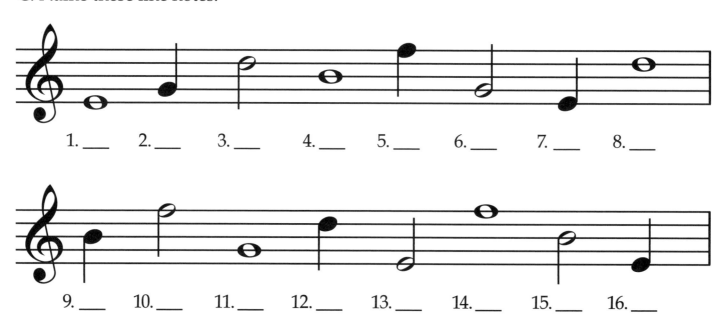

1. ___   2. ___   3. ___   4. ___   5. ___   6. ___   7. ___   8. ___

9. ___   10. ___   11. ___   12. ___   13. ___   14. ___   15. ___   16. ___

You are ready for **Lines and Spaces Note Speller** (KP23).

RH 4 begins on ___.

LH 1 begins on ___.
LH 5 begins on ___.

Wind Chimes

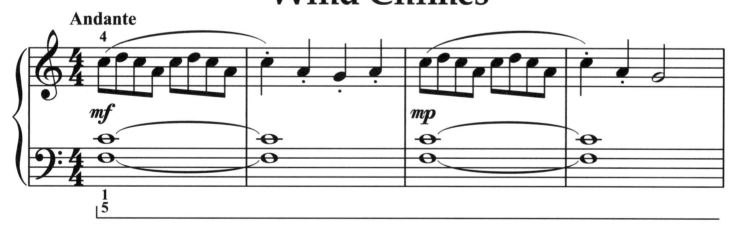

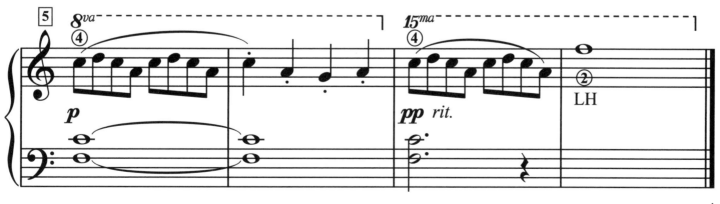

I Chord and V7 Chord in G

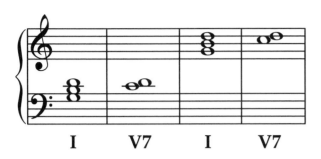

I   V7   I   V7

Team Cheer

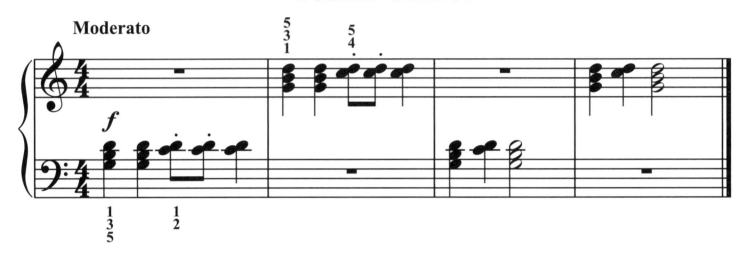

Hot Air Balloon Ride

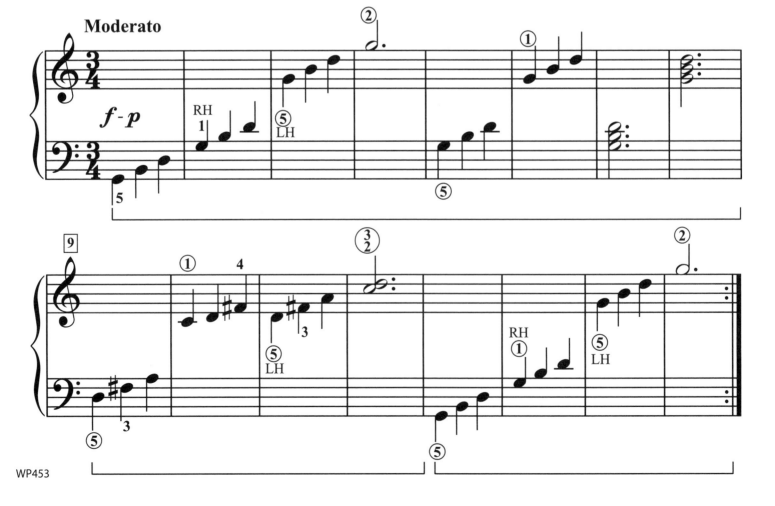

Out to Sea

Andante

German Folk Tune

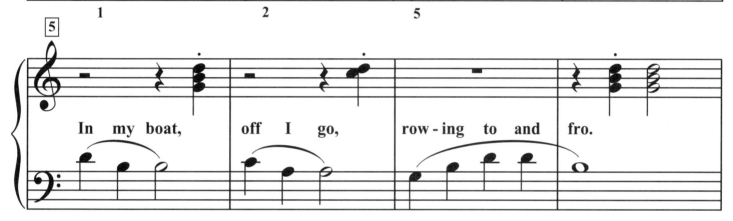

Pad-dling on, out to sea, Cool wind blow-ing right thru me,

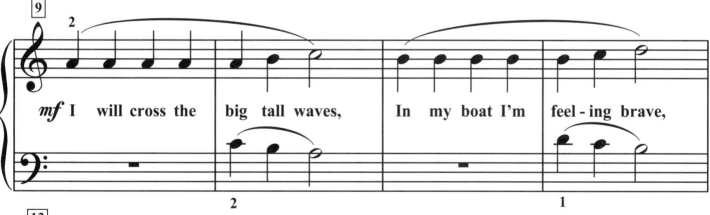

In my boat, off I go, row-ing to and fro.

I will cross the big tall waves, In my boat I'm feel-ing brave,

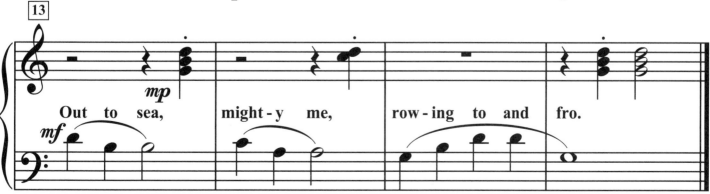

Out to sea, might-y me, row-ing to and fro.

*The left hand has the melody. Listen for soft right hand chords.

Treble Clef Space Notes

A. Write the note names inside the noteheads.

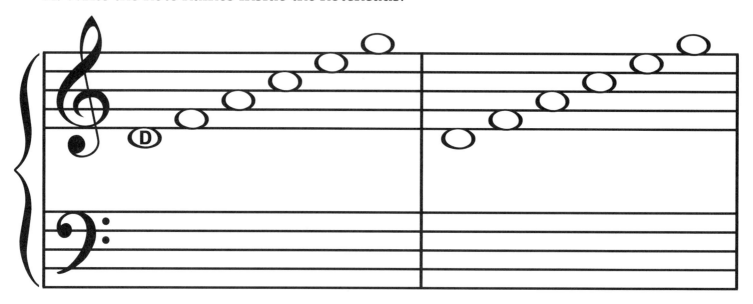

B. Write a saying for the treble clef space notes to help you remember the letter names. An example: **D**ucks **FACE G**eese (The treble 𝄞 space notes on the staff spell the word "face.")

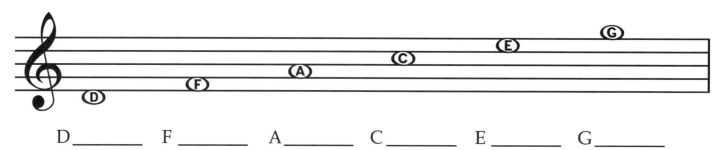

D_____   F _____   A_____   C_____   E _____   G_____

C. Name these space notes.

1. __   2. __   3. __   4. __   5. __   6. __   7. __   8. __

___

ACCOMPANIMENT for "Gavotte"

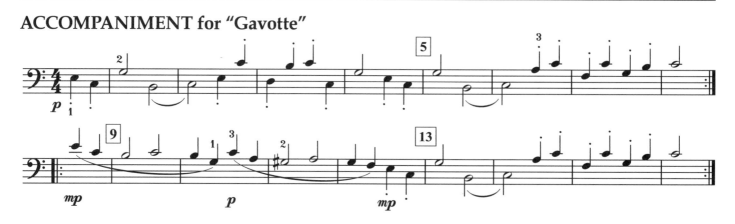

RH 1 begins on ___.
LH 3 begins on ___.

Gavotte

Georg Philipp Telemann
(Arranged)

Allegretto

mp Please do lis-ten as you play this mus- ic, You'll hear fan- cy, clev-er phras- es. Writ-ten

in the ear-ly six-teen hun-dreds, Still a clas-sic for to- day. Te- le-mann com-
mf

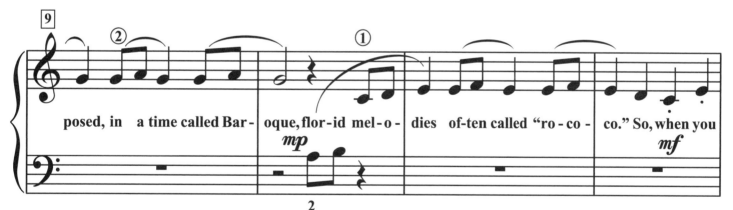

posed, in a time called Bar- oque, flor-id mel-o - dies of-ten called "ro-co- co." So, when you
mp *mf*

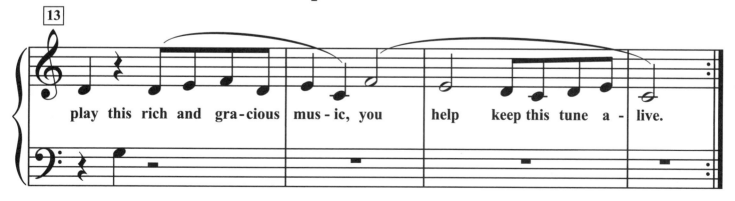

play this rich and gra-cious mus- ic, you help keep this tune a - live.

Play all chords softly throughout this piece.

RH 1 begins on ___.
LH 4 begins on ___.

Surfing

Scottish Folk Tune

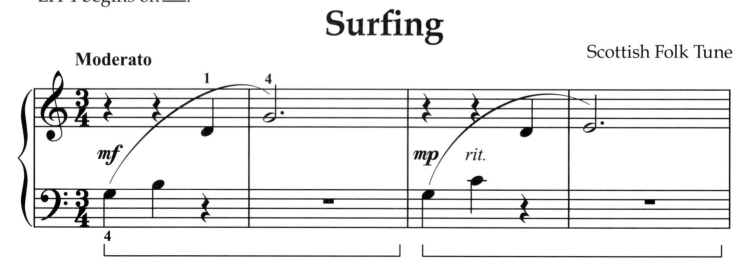

43

WP453

Single Eighth Note:    ## Eighth Rest: ♪

♪ = 1/2 beat in **2/4**, **3/4**, and **4/4**.

♪ ♪ = ♫ = ♩ = 1 beat

♪ = 1/2 beat

Example: Clap and count aloud.
2/4 ♪ ♪ ♪ ♪ | ♫ ♪ ♪ ‖
    1 + 2 +   1 + 2 +

A. Trace and shade each note or rest, then draw two more.

B. Write the counts under the rhythm, then clap and count it aloud.

1 + 2 + _____

_____

C. Write the number of beats each note receives
to complete these "music math" problems.

♪ + ♪ + ♩.

☐ + ☐ + ☐ = ☐ beats

♫ + ♪ + ♪ + ♩

☐ + ☐ + ☐ + ☐ = ☐ beats

LH 1 begins on ___.
RH 5 begins on ___.

Stormy Skies

Moderato

mp 1. Rain is com - ing, skies grow dark - er, not a sin - gle sound, calm be - fore the storm.
mf 2. What a down-pour, thun - der, light-ning, sud den-ly it's passed, no more rain to - day.

8va

Fine

Lit - tle rain drops hit the pave-ment see the storm be - gin to form.
Streets are wet with scat-tered pud - dles storm-y skies move on their way.

mp

mf

D.C. al Fine

f

mp

Write the counts on the gray line, then clap and count the rhythm aloud.

1   +

RH 3 begins on ___.

RH 1 begins on ___.

LH 1 begins on ___.

The State Fair

Allegretto

WP453

48

Review

A. Name each interval (**2nd**, **3rd**, **4th**, or **5th**).

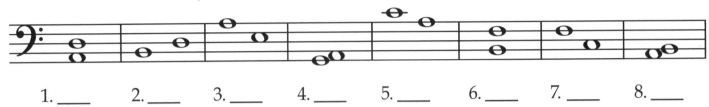

1. ___ 2. ___ 3. ___ 4. ___ 5. ___ 6. ___ 7. ___ 8. ___

B. Write the counts, then clap and count the rhythm aloud.

1 +

Tiger Twins

Note Review

A. Name the notes.

B. Write the number of each note on the matching key below.

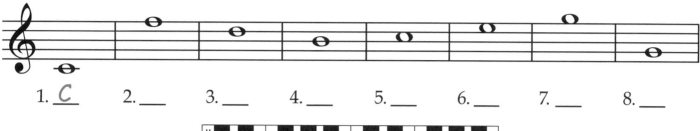

1. _C_ 2. __ 3. __ 4. __ 5. __ 6. __ 7. __ 8. __

Alpine Skiing

Andante

Play both hands 8va higher the first time.

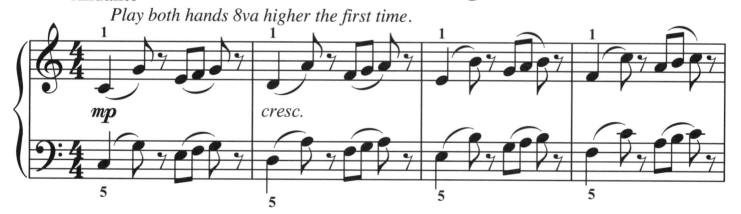

Dotted Quarter Note

Count: "**Quar** - ter dot"

or

Count: "1 & 2"

A dot after any note is equal to half the value of the note.

 + · =

1 + ½ = 1 ½ beats

= 2 beats

= 2 beats

A dotted quarter note equals a quarter note tied to an eighth note.

Write the counts, then clap and count the rhythm aloud.

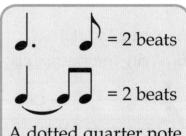

London Bridge

Moderato

English Folk Song

Lon - don Bridge is | fall-ing down, | fall-ing down, | fall-ing down,

Lon - don Bridge is | fall-ing down, | my fair | lad - y.

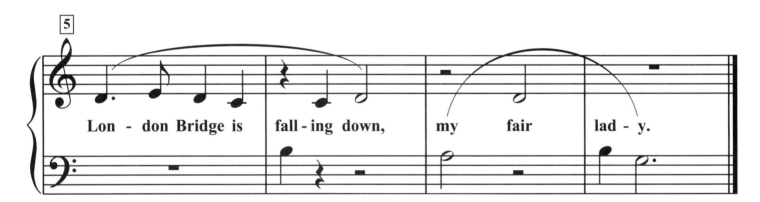

Deck the Hall

Old Welsh Air

Allegretto

cross over

Deck the hall with boughs of hol - ly, fa-la-la-la-la, la - la-la-la.

D.S. al Fine is an abbreviation for *Dal Segno al Fine*. It means to return to the *Segno* (sign 𝄋) and play again until the *Fine* (end).

Alouette

French-Canadian Folk Song

Allegretto

mf

A - lou-et - te, **gen-tille A-lou-e - te,**

A - lou-et - te, **Je te plu-me-rai.** *Fine* **Je te plu-me-rai la tête,**

Je te plu-me-rai la tête. *f* **Et la tête, et la tête,** *prepare* **A-lou-ett', oh!** *D.S. al Fine*

prepare

WP453

Silent Movie Music

RH 2 begins on ___.
LH 3 begins on ___.

Fly Away

English Folk Tune

ACCOMPANIMENT (Student plays one octave higher.)

Treble 𝄞 and Bass 𝄢 Line Notes

A. Write the names of the line notes three times.

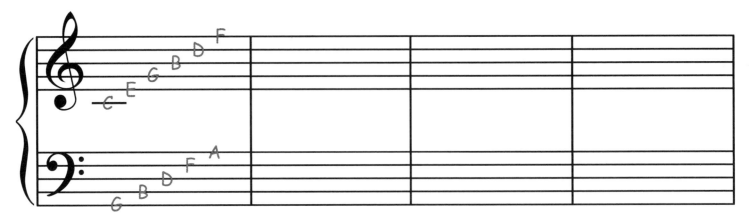

B. Name the notes to form words.

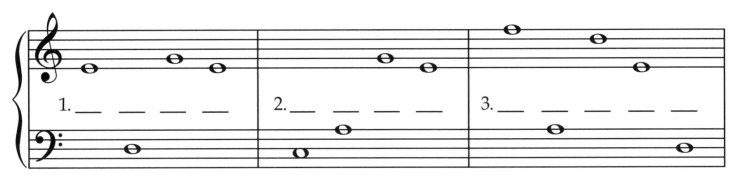

1. __ __ __ __
2. __ __ __ __
3. __ __ __ __ __

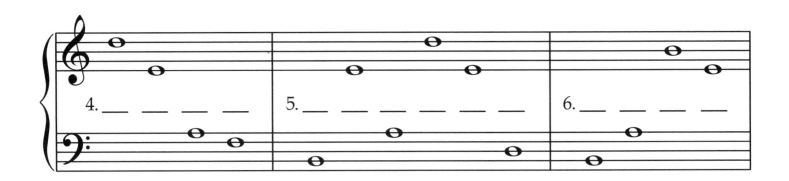

4. __ __ __ __
5. __ __ __ __ __
6. __ __ __ __

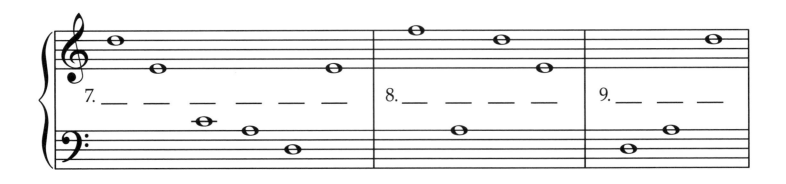

7. __ __ __ __ __ __
8. __ __ __ __
9. __ __ __ __

Treble 𝄞 and Bass 𝄢 Space Notes

A. Write the names of the line notes three times.

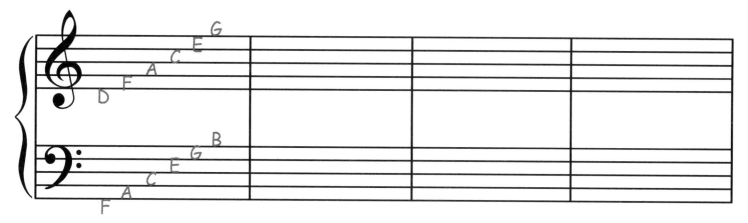

B. Name the notes to form words.

1. __ __ __ __ __ __ __

2. __ __ __ __

3. __ __ __ __

4. __ __ __ __

5. __ __ __ __ __

6. __ __ __ __ __ __

7. __ __ __ __

8. __ __ __ __ __ __ __

9. __ __ __ __ __

When the Saints Go Marching In

American Gospel Hymn

A. Trace the clef signs and grand staves in exercises 1 and 2.
B. For exercise 3, draw the grand staff, including the clef signs.

1.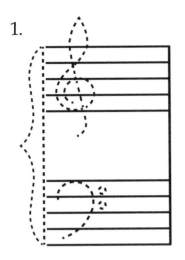

2.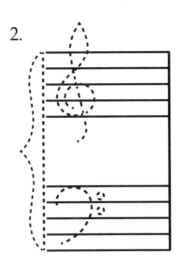

3.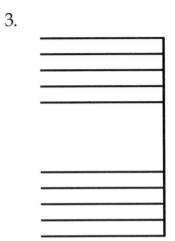

Shepherd's Song

Ludwig van Beethoven
Arr. from *Symphony No. 6* ("Pastorale")

Allegretto

Cinco de Mayo

Accent
The symbol > is an accent mark.
When placed over or under a note,
it indicates to play the note(s) louder .

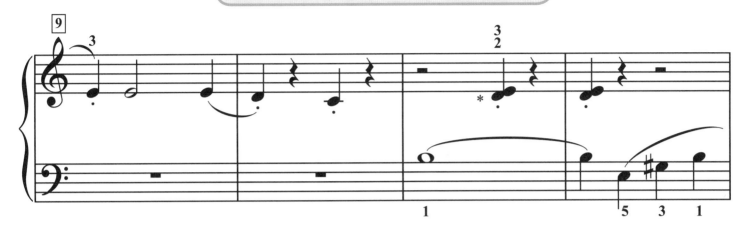

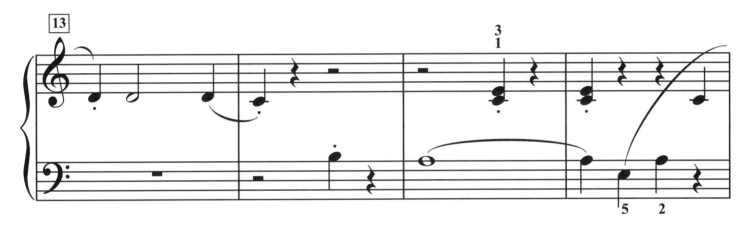

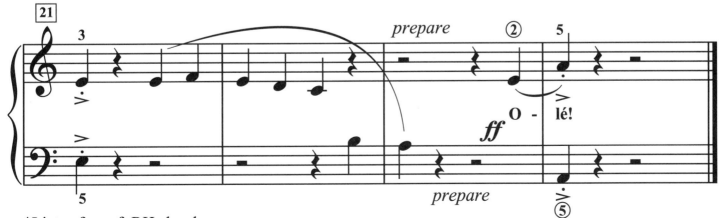

prepare

prepare

O - lé!

*Listen for soft RH chords.

F 5-Finger Position

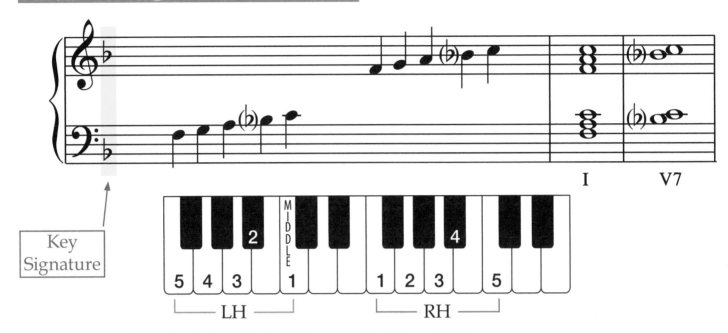

Key Signature

The set of sharps or flats at the beginning of each staff
is the **key signature**. It tells you:
1. The notes to be played as sharps or flats in the piece.
2. The key of the piece.

Name the chords (**I** or **V7**), then play *Etude in F*.

Etude in F

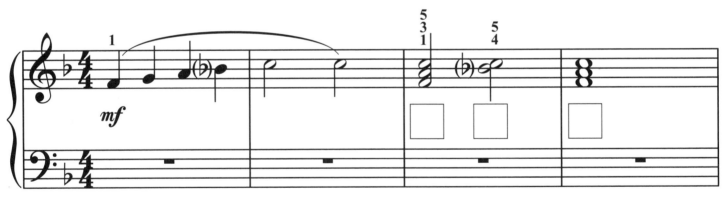

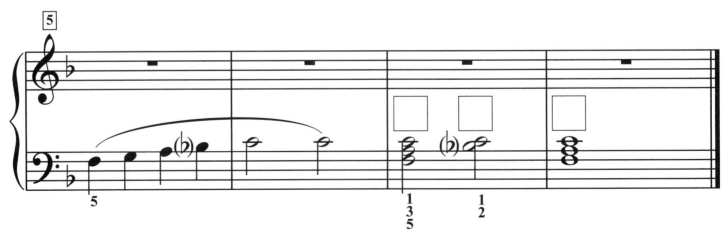

WP453

Marching Band

Marching tempo

Hear the big band play.

March-ing down this way.

Horns and drums and clar - i - nets will play for us to - day.

*Listen for soft LH chords throughout.

Group 1 Keys: C, G, F

You have learned to play in three keys: C, G, and F. These three keys are called the **Group 1 keys** because they all have the same look and feel in their **I chords**. Each **I chord** has only **white keys**.

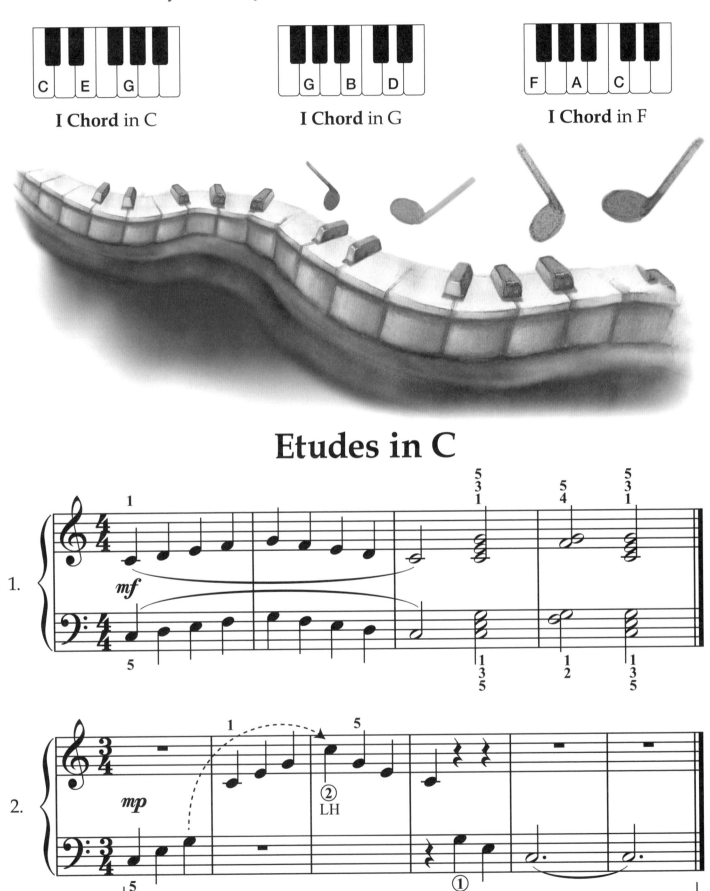

I Chord in C   **I Chord** in G   **I Chord** in F

Etudes in C

Etudes in G

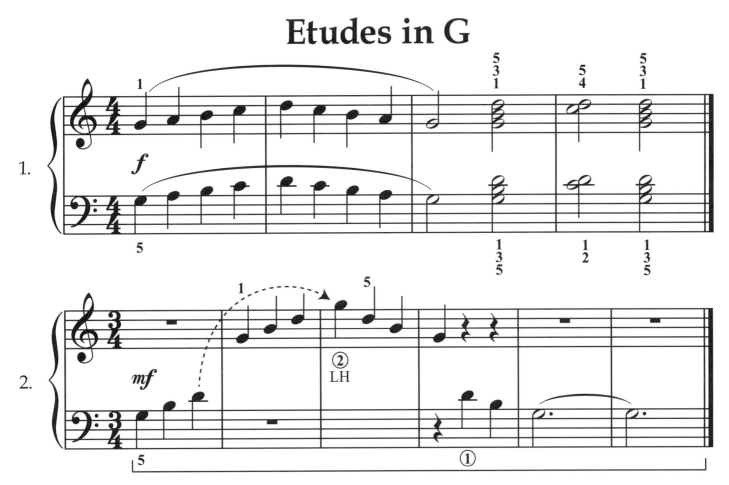

1.

2.

*The key signature is omitted here for the Key of G because there is no F♯ in the 5-finger position.
This key signature will be introduced in Level 2A when the full G Major scale is shown.

Etudes in F

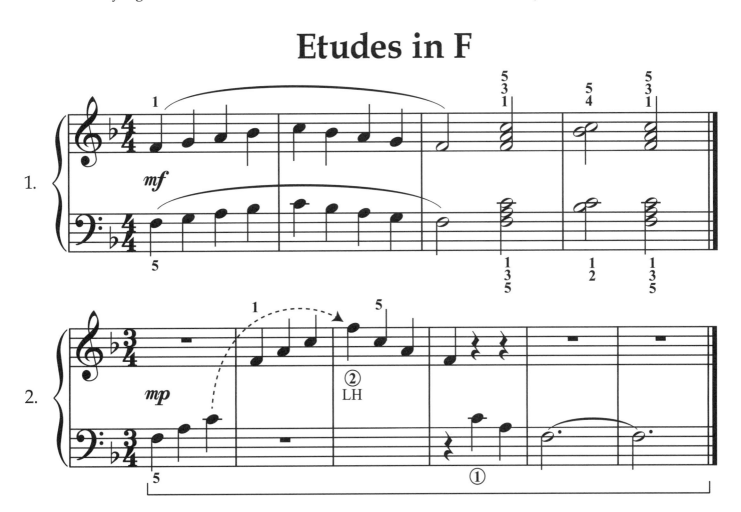

1.

2.

Harp Melody

Harps
Like the piano, the harp has many strings. Performers pluck the strings with their fingers to make music. Harps vary in size; small harps are held in the lap, others stand on a table, and the largest concert harps stand on the floor. A musician who plays folk music on the harp is called a "harper," while classical performers call themselves "harpists."

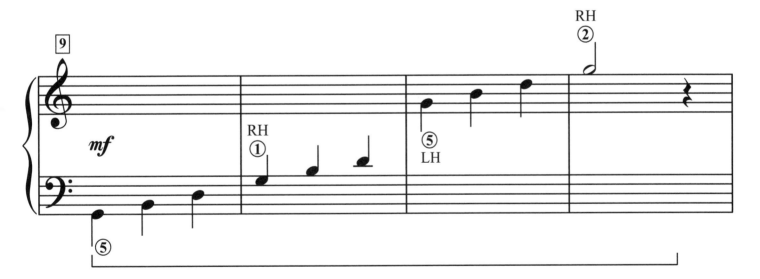

Ode to Joy

Beethoven
Theme from *Symphony No. 9*
(Arranged)

Ludwig van Beethoven (1770-1827) is one of Germany's most famous composers. His music has a special character of strength and form. Although Beethoven became deaf during his later years, he continued to compose some of his finest music. The *Symphony No. 9*, composed late in Beethoven's life, is one of his best-known works.

The Star Spangled Banner

Words by
Francis Scott Key

U.S. National Anthem
John Stafford Smith

*Fermata (⌢) Hold the note(s) under a fermata sign longer than the original time value.

Certificate of Achievement

This certifies that

has completed Level 1B
of

Bastien® New Traditions

and is promoted to Level 2A.

This certificate is given in recognition of this significant achievement!

Teacher's Signature

Date